Better Management Skills

This highly popular range of inexpensive paperbacks covers all areas of basic management. Practical, easy to read and instantly accessible, these guides will help managers to improve their business or communication skills. Those marked * are available on audio cassette.

The books in this series can be tailored to specific company requirements. For further details, please contact the publisher, Kogan Page, telephone 0171-278 0433, fax 0171-837 6348.

Be a Successful Supervisor
Be Positive
Business Creativity
Business Etiquette
Coaching Your Employees
Conducting Effective Interviews
Counselling Your Staff
Creative Decision-making
Creative Thinking in Business
Delegating for Results
Effective Employee Participation
Effective Meeting Skills
Effective Performance Appraisals*
Effective Presentation Skills
Empowerment
First Time Supervisor
Get Organised!
Goals and Goal Setting
How to Communicate Effectively*
How to Develop a Positive Attitude*
How to Develop Assertiveness
How to Manage Organisational
    Change
How to Motivate People*
How to Understand Financial
    Statements
How to Write a Staff Manual
Improving Employee Performance
Improving Relations at Work
Keeping Customers for Life
Leadership Skills for Women

Learning to Lead
Make Every Minute Count*
Making TQM Work
Managing Cultural Diversity at
    Work
Managing Disagreement
    Constructively
Managing Organisational Change
Managing Part-time Employees
Managing Quality Customer Service
Managing Your Boss
Marketing for Success
Memory Skills in Business
Mentoring
Office Management
Personnel Testing
Productive Planning
Project Management
Quality Customer Service
Rate Your Skills as a Manager
Sales Training Basics
Self-managing Teams
Selling Professionally
Successful Negotiation
Successful Presentation Skills
Successful Telephone Techniques
Systematic Problem-solving and
    Decision-making
Team Building
Training Methods that Work
The Woman Manager

TEAM
BUILDING

An Exercise in Leadership

Second Edition

Robert B Maddux

KOGAN
PAGE

Copyright © Crisp Publications Inc 1986, 1988

First published in the United States of America in 1986
by Crisp Publications Inc, 95 First Street,
Los Altos, California 94022, USA
Second Edition 1988

First published in Great Britain in 1988
by Kogan Page Ltd, 120 Pentonville Road, London N1 9JN
Second edition 1994

Reprinted 1994, 1996, 1997

British Library Cataloguing in Publication Data

A CIP record for this book is available from the British Library.

ISBN 0-7494-1411-1

Typeset by DP Photosetting, Aylesbury, Bucks
Printed and bound in Great Britain by
Clays Ltd, St Ives plc

Contents

Contents

Preface

In all economic systems, people must produce the goods and services that are essential to life. How well, and how much they produce depends on their knowledge; skill; creativity; commitment; attitude; the technology employed; and finally the quality of those who manage them.

Typically, people work in small groups which have common or related functions. Each person in such a group has an individual aspiration, level of skill, and attitude towards the task. Since people think, feel and respond according to their individuality, they sometimes do not consider the benefits of supporting and cooperating with others to achieve a common goal. This can be seen at the first practice of any school athletic team. Some players have considerable talent, others are less skilful. Ultimately the group will not have much success until they are motivated to work towards a common goal. A skilled coach will be able to pool their talent and train them to play together, compensating for individual strengths and weaknesses.

Similarly, in a work environment, the results achieved are seldom the outcome of one individual's talent. Each person is influenced by the attitude and action of co-workers and managers. If the influence of the work environment is positive, a person tends to be productive. The same is true for a group of workers. When the influence is negative, both individuals and groups tend to be less productive.

This book is devoted to teaching concepts which make work positive and productive. It contains principles by which a group can be transformed into a team. The concepts are easily understood but their application takes dedication and effort.

Robert B Maddux

CHAPTER 1

Which Objectives Do You Want to Achieve

Objectives give us a sense of direction, a definition of what we plan to accomplish, and a sense of fulfilment when they are achieved. Tick the objectives that are important to you. This book will help you to achieve them.

I hope to:

- [ ] Be able to explain the difference between a group and a team.

- [ ] Learn how to recognise situations that call for team rather than group behaviour.

- [ ] Learn how to build a team from a group.

- [ ] Be able to understand and apply leadership techniques.

- [ ] Enjoy the personal and organisational rewards of team behaviour.

CHAPTER 2
Groups versus Teams

Groups are fundamental units of organisation

From the beginning of time people have formed groups. Groups provide the basis for family living, protection, waging war, government, recreation and work. Group behaviour has ranged from total chaos to dramatic success, but it is increasingly evident that groups enjoy their greatest success when they become more productive units called teams.

Managers in many organisations seem content with group performance. This is often because they have not thought beyond what is being accomplished to what might be achieved under slightly different circumstances. Other leaders using the same number of people, doing similar tasks with the same technology, somehow manage to improve productivity dramatically by establishing a climate where people are willing to give their best and work together in teams.

A comparison of teams and groups is shown below; tick ☑ the characteristics representative of the unit of which you are currently a part.

Groups	Teams
☐ Members think they are grouped together for administrative purposes only. Individuals work independently, sometimes at cross purposes with others.	☐ Members recognise their interdependence and understand both personal and team goals are best accomplished with mutual support. Time is not wasted · struggling over territory or seeking personal gain at the expense of others.

☐ Members tend to focus on themselves because they are not sufficiently involved in planning the unit's objectives. They approach their job simply hired hands.

☐ Members feel a sense of ownership for their jobs and unit because they are committed to goals they helped to establish.

☐ Members are told what to do rather than being asked what the best approach would be. Suggestions are not encouraged.

☐ Members contribute to the organisation's success by applying their unique talent and knowledge to team objectives.

☐ Members distrust the motives of colleagues because they do not understand the role of other members. Expressions of opinion or disagreement are considered divisive or unsupportive.

☐ Members work in a climate of trust and are encouraged to express openly ideas, opinions, disagreements and feelings. Questions are welcomed.

☐ Members are so cautious about what they say that real understanding is not possible. Game playing may occur and communication traps be set to catch the unwary.

☐ Members practise open and honest communication. They make an effort to understand each other's point of view.

☐ Members may receive good training but are limited in applying it to the job by the supervisor or other group members.

☐ Members are encouraged to develop skills and apply what they learn on the job. They receive the support of the team.

☐ Members find themselves in conflict situations which they do not know how to resolve. Their supervisor may put off intervention until serious damage is done.

☐ Members recognise conflict is a normal aspect of human interaction but they view such situations as an opportunity for new ideas and creativity. They work to resolve conflict quickly and constructively.

☐ Members may or may not participate in decisions affecting the team. Conformity often appears more important than positive results.

☐ Members participate in decisions affecting the team but understand their leader must make a final ruling whenever the team cannot decide, or an emergency exists. Positive results, not conformity, are the goal.

CHAPTER 3
Group Managers versus Team Leaders

Team leaders exhibit styles from those who are content to manage a group. These styles are shaped by each person's life experience and the values they have adopted over the years.

Given today's rapid rate of organisational change, and the changing needs of people, it is important for those 'in charge' to re-evaluate and modify their styles on a regular basis. This is the only way they can make the adaptations necessary to continue to be effective.

See how team-centred leadership differs from group-centred management on the facing page – then make a commitment to creating and supporting a team effort.

Plan how you will make any needed changes in your style and evaluate the results carefully. Keep making adjustments until you achieve the desired results. Stay on the alert for additional ways to improve your leadership.

Differences between group-centred managers and team-centred managers

Identify the qualities which best describe you at this time with a ☑

Group-centred	**Team-centred**
☐ Overriding concern to meet current goals inhibits thought about what might be accomplished through reorganising to enhance member contributions.	☐ Current goals are taken in stride. Can be a visionary about what the people can achieve as a team. Can share vision and act accordingly.

☐ Reactive to upper management, peers and employees. Find it easier to go along with the crowd.

☐ Proactive in most relationships. Exhibits personal style. Can stimulate excitement and action. Inspires teamwork and mutual support.

☐ Willing to involve people in planning and problem-solving to some extent but within limits.

☐ Can get people involved and committed. Makes it easy for others to see opportunities for teamwork. Allows people to perform.

☐ Resents or distrusts employees who know their jobs better than the manager.

☐ Looks for people who want to excel and can work constructively with others. Feels role is to encourage and facilitate this behaviour.

☐ Sees group problem-solving as a waste of time, or an abdication of managerial responsibility.

☐ Considers problem-solving the responsiblity of team members.

☐ Controls information and communicates only what group members need or want to know.

☐ Communicates fully and openly. Welcomes questions. Allows the team to do its own information filtering.

☐ Ignores conflict between staff members or with other groups.

☐ Mediates conflict before it becomes destructive.

☐ Sometimes slow to recognise individual or group achievements.

☐ Makes an effort to see that both individual and team accomplishments are recognised at the right time in an appropriate manner.

☐ Sometimes modifies group agreements to suit personal convenience.

☐ Keeps commitments and expects the same in return.

Increased productivity is the by-product of teamwork

When productive teams are compared with less productive groups, there are some important differences involving the application of team concepts. Here is an example:

A study was made of 20 coal mines operating in the same geological structure, drawing from the same labour pool, and subject to the same regulations. Productivity was measured in tons of coal produced per employee per shift.

The mine with the highest productivity delivered 242 tons per employee contrasted with the lowest which mined 58 tons per employee. The other mines were somewhere in between.

Conclusions from this study were summarised as follows: 'The primary difference was the way in which management worked with the employees. The most productive mine provided employees with significantly more individual responsibility and involvement in goal setting and problem-solving.'

CHAPTER 4

Team Building Concepts Can Be Applied in any Organisation

A diverse group formed each year to compete in a sport is an excellent example of team building. Groups develop into 'teams' when their common purpose is understood by all the members. In effective teams each member plays an assigned role using his or her talent to the best advantage. When the members integrate their skills to accentuate strengths and minimise weaknesses, team objectives are usually achieved. When, on the other hand, groups play as individuals, they usually fail. Most wins or losses are the result of 'teamwork'. In sports, feedback is often immediate. If teamwork is lacking, good managers can identify where the problems are, and initiate corrective action in order to change things until the desired results are achieved.

Like their athletic counterparts, groups organised to perform business, community and governmental functions can achieve far more when they work as 'teams'. Unfortunately, many leaders fail to recognise and apply the same principles as they would coaching a sport. In a work organisation they do not understand how to transform their group into a productive team. One reason may be that feedback in the form of results is not as quick or dramatic as in athletics. Problems can go unnoticed and corrective action, if taken, can be slow in coming.

Effective teamwork knows no level. It is as important among top executives as it is among middle managers, first line supervisors or the rank and file. The absence of teamwork at any level (or between levels) will limit organisational effectiveness and can eventually kill an organisation.

It requires effort to establish and maintain teamwork

If a leader does not place a high value on teamwork it will not occur. Teamwork takes conscious effort to develop and continuous effort to maintain, but the rewards can be great. Consider the examples on the next page.

CHAPTER 5

What Can Team Building Do for Me?

Leaders sometimes assign a low priority to team building because they have not considered the advantages that can accrue from a well executed team effort.

Below are some results of team performance. Tick ☑ those you would like to achieve.

☐ Realistic, achievable goals can be established for the team and individual members because those responsible for doing the work contribute to their construction.

☐ Employees and leaders commit to support each other to make the team successful.

☐ Team members understand one another's priorities and help or support when difficulties arise.

☐ Communication is open. The discussion of new ideas, improved work methods, articulation of problems and concerns is encouraged.

☐ Problem-solving is more effective because the expertise of the team is available.

☐ Performance feedback is more meaningful because team members understand what is expected and can monitor their performance against expectations.

☐ Conflict is understood as normal and viewed as an opportunity to solve problems. Through open discussion it can be resolved before it becomes destructive.

☐ Balance is maintained between group productivity and the satisfaction of personal team members' needs.

☐ The team is recognised for outstanding results, as are individuals for their personal contributions.

☐ Members are encouraged to test their abilities and try out ideas. This becomes infectious and stimulates individuals to become stronger performers.

☐ Team members recognise the importance of disciplined work habits and conform their behaviour to meet team standards.

☐ Learning to work effectively as a team in one unit is good preparation for working as a team with other units. It is also good preparation for advancement.

Teamwork and productivity go hand in hand.

Your attitude will make a big difference in team building

When the concept of team building is understood and applied at all levels in an organisation it becomes much easier to transform groups into teams throughout the organisation.

It is to any leader's advantage, however, to develop a team whether others are doing so or not. A positive attitude towards team building is essential.

Check your attitude by completing the exercise on the next page.

CHAPTER 6
Attitudes of an Effective Team Builder

The following attitudes support team building. This scale will help to identify your strengths, and determine areas where improvement would be beneficial. Circle the number that best reflects where you fall on the scale. The higher the number, the more the characteristic describes you. When you have finished, total the numbers circled in the space provided.

1. When I select employees I choose those who can meet the job requirements and work well with others.

   7 6 5 4 3 2 1

2. I give employees a sense of ownership by involving them in goal setting, problem-solving and productivity improvement activities.

   7 6 5 4 3 2 1

3. I try to provide team spirit by encouraging people to work together and to support one another in activities that are related.

   7 6 5 4 3 2 1

4. I talk with people openly and honestly and encourage the same kind of communication in return.

   7 6 5 4 3 2 1

5. I keep agreements with my people because their trust is essential to my leadership.

   7 6 5 4 3 2 1

6. I help team members to get to know each other so they will understand their colleagues and be aware of others' abilities.

   7 6 5 4 3 2 1

7. I ensure employees have the necessary   7 6 5 4 3 2 1
   training to do their job and know how it
   is to be applied.

8. I understand that conflict within groups   7 6 5 4 3 2 1
   is normal, but work to resolve it quickly
   and fairly before it can become
   destructive.

9. I believe people will perform as a team   7 6 5 4 3 2 1
   when they know what is expected and
   what benefits will accrue.

10. I am willing to replace members who   7 6 5 4 3 2 1
    cannot or will not meet reasonable
    standards after appropriate coaching.

TOTAL _____

A score between 60 and 70 indicates a positive attitude towards people and the type of attitude needed to build and maintain a strong team. A score between 40 and 59 is acceptable and with reasonable effort, team building should be possible for you. If you scored below 40, you need to examine your attitude carefully in light of current management philosophy.

Case studies help to provide insights you may not already possess. Four case problems are included in this book.

The first case (on the next page) will help you to understand the importance of learning and applying team building concepts.

CHAPTER 7
Can This Supervisor Be Saved?

Case 1

Marilyn has been supervisor to five employees for about three months. It is her first supervisory assignment, and she has had little training.

Although each employee has a different job with its own standards, the tasks are interrelated and the success of the unit depends upon a cooperative effort. Marilyn has worked hard to assign tasks, set deadlines and solve problems in order to achieve the desired results. However, the poor skills of two employees, and the constant bickering within the group have caused delays and personal frustration for everyone. Marilyn would like to spend more time with her employees but paperwork and reporting seem to consume most of her time. She has also begun to stay in her office more recently because of the hostility between the employees. Group productivity has fallen below expectations, and Marilyn is increasingly afraid she may be fired.

What might Marilyn do to save her job and turn the performance of the unit around?

_____

_____

_____

_____

_____

Check your answer with those of the author on page 83.

Team building can be compared with cricket

- A skilled manager has responsibility to help select the players, coordinate the team's effort, and oversee the playing of the game.
- Players must know their jobs, have the skill to do them well, and be committed to make a contribution to the team.
- To beat the competition requires a game plan.
- Players and the manager must communicate with each another, trust and suport one another, and resolve their differences in a constructive manner.
- Self-control must be exercised by each player or, in its absence, be imposed by the manager.
- There must be a reward system that meets both the needs of the team and the personal needs of individual players.

Be a self-starter

If you are waiting for someone in higher management to tell you to build a team, you may be limiting the success of your unit and yourself. A thinking, proactive manager will not wait for a directive from above. Instead, he or she will begin immediately to make a concerted effort to develop solid management skills. The next few pages will help you to determine how much work you have to do to become an effective team leader.

CHAPTER 8
Become an Effective Planner

Team need to know why they exist, what they are supposed to accomplish and who else is involved. If these areas are fuzzy, frustration is the result. Team members expect their leader to know the direction they are to take, and how they are to coordinate with other groups to reach their goals. To accomplish this, effective planning is required.

Planning is the thinking that precedes the work. If planning is not done, time and effort are usually wasted. Effective planning includes the following elements. Tick your proficiency level for each.

	Do well	Should improve
1. Interpreting goals which are passed down as the result of planning at higher levels.	☐	☐
2. Articulating organisational needs (including those of the team) into team goals and objectives.	☐	☐
3. Formulating implementation plans by examining alternatives and selecting activities which lead to successful results.	☐	☐
4. Identifying resources needed to achieve goals (people, time, money, materials and facilities) and ensuring they are available.	☐	☐
5. Establishing deadlines and target completion dates.	☐	☐
6. Determining standards of performance and how results will be measured.	☐	☐

Employees can make important contributions to planning once they become committed to the process. If you coordinate planning well, your team leadership will be much more effective. If you need to improve – DO IT NOW!

CHAPTER 9
Strengthen Your Organising Skills

Leaders must be well organised and capable of helping the team organise itself to accomplish established goals.

One of the strengths of a good leader is the ability to see a future for the organisation that is better in some important ways than what currently exists.

This view must then be communicated in such a way that employees can organise their resources to achieve the desired results.

Once planning is underway, organisation becomes important. Resources – people, capital, raw materials, and technology – must be coordinated effectively to achieve team goals.

Team members look to the leader for direction and the allocation of resources. If organisation is poor, the group will become confused, discouraged, argumentative, uncooperative and defensive. Teamwork will be impossible.

Some key aspects of organisation are listed below. Tick your proficiency in each.

	Do well	Should improve
1. I can divide work into logical tasks and groupings.	☐	☐
2. I know how to secure the resources required to achieve goals.	☐	☐
3. I am comfortable assigning tasks, resources and responsibility to team members on the basis of functions and skills.	☐	☐

	Do well	Should improve
4. I can establish guidelines in order to coordinate activities between team members and other groups involved with the outcome.	☐	☐
5. I make it a practice to design information systems which ensure appropriate feedback as the work progresses.	☐	☐
6. I can establish communications networks to ensure there is a free flow of information up, down, and across organisational lines.	☐	☐

Employees can make important contributions to the organising process because of their knowledge and experience. Employee involvement can enhance teamwork and efficiency. The better your organisational skills, the stronger you should be as a leader. If you need to improve – DO IT NOW!

Make an effort to understand people and their needs

Establishing yourself as a strong leader requires an understanding of people and what motivates them. Those who understand can create a working climate in which team members can meet individual needs while achieving team goals.

Understanding what motivates individual employees requires time and effort but the results are worth it. The material on the next page will help you to determine how good you are at building a climate which motivates employees to be successful.

CHAPTER 10
Build a Motivating Climate

People work for a variety of reasons. What is important to one person may have little significance to another. Motivation is personal and supervisors must get to know individual employees in order to learn what motivates them. Some people work for basic survival needs, while others are seeking security. Some work to fulfil ego satisfaction, or something even deeper.

A supervisor must be sensitive to recognise these employee needs, and design ways to meet them while achieving the goals of the organistion. No single technique works for everyone. When the following elements are combined, however, both individual and team success is possible. Tick your proficiency below.

I am proficient at:	Do well	Should improve
1. Ensuring each employee knows what is expected and how performance will be measured.	☐	☐
2. Getting to know employees as individuals to learn their needs.	☐	☐
3. Providing the training and supervisory assistance necessary for each employee to achieve mutually established objectives.	☐	☐
4. Providing the resources required to perform the job.	☐	☐
5. Guiding and encouraging personal development for individual employees.	☐	☐
6. Recognising and rewarding good performance and correcting or eliminating poor performance when it occurs.	☐	☐

Good leaders know how to build a motivating climate. If you need to improve – DO IT NOW!

Control is essential to achieving goals

A supervisor, like a sports team manager, must keep the game plan in mind. As the action progresses, modifying and adjusting this plan may be necessary to keep the team focused and on target. This process is called controlling. Check your approach to control on the next page.

CHAPTER 11

Establish a Control System That Will Ensure Goal Achievement

Once a project has begun, a control system is needed to make sure it will progress according to plan, and the ultimate objective be achieved. Controls should be established during the planning process, and be as simple as possible.

Once a control system is in place, the leader and the team can compare what is happening with what was expected. Based on the ongoing results, it may be necessary to revise the objective, modify the plan, reorganise, take some added motivational steps or other appropriate action. Some important aspects of controlling are listed below. Indicate your proficiency with each by ticking the appropriate box.

I normally:	Do well	Should improve
1. Establish control elements as part of the project plan.	☐	☐
2. Set up time schedules and checkpoints to measure progress.	☐	☐
3. Encourage feedback from team members throughout the project.	☐	☐
4. Evaluate problems or deviations from plans, and then construct a new action plan which keeps the schedule and is appropriate.	☐	☐
5. Adjust objectives, plans, resources or motivational factors as required to meet the organisational goals.	☐	☐
6. Communicate progress and plan changes to those who need to know.	☐	☐

In a team situation, employees should, by virtue of their involvement, do much of the controlling. If you need to improve your skills in this area – DO IT NOW!

The case study on the next page will give you a chance to apply what you have learned.

CHAPTER 12
Which Supervisor Would You Prefer?

Case 2

Moira and Jeff have just been promoted to their first supervisory positions. Both have had considerable experience as senior micro-technicians prior to the promotion. Moira and Jeff shared plans for making the transition from technician to supervisor one day during lunch.

Moira volunteered that she plans to concentrate on defining the work that needs to be done, and then provide her employees with precise goals and standards. Because of her experience and knowledge, she will also prepare a detailed performance plan for each employee. She feels this approach will ensure the goals are met while giving her the control she needs to get the job done.

Jeff responded by saying he had already secured his manager's agreement to take a supervisory skills course to ensure he understood the management process. In the meantime, how-ever, Jeff indicated he plans to involve his group in day-to-day planning, organising and problem-solving. Jeff is confident of his ability but feels every member of his staff is competent, and can make important contributions to the group's effectiveness. He also feels that individuals need the satisfaction that comes from being involved in a project.

Which of these supervisors would you rather work for?

_____

_____

_____

Compare your response with the author's on page 83.

CHAPTER 13
Select Qualified People

Human resources are the most critical part of any organisation's success. Good people help to ensure profitability, productivity, growth and long-term survival. You simply cannot survive without qualified people. As a team leader it is essential for you that these people learn to work together. Some critical elements in employee selection and placement are listed below. Indicate how well you perform by ticking the appropriate box.

	Do well	Should improve
1. I analyse job requirements thoroughly before beginning the selection process.	☐	☐
2. I always probe for objective evidence of an applicant's skills: knowledge; past successes and failures; dependability; attitude towards work and co-workers; supervision and customers.	☐	☐
3. I describe my idea of teamwork to applicants and ask them to assess how they would work under team conditions.	☐	☐
4. I make sure each applicant understands the job requirements and expected standards of performance.	☐	☐
5. I evaluate facts carefully and avoid making premature conclusions or stereotyping while making a selection decision.	☐	☐
6. People I take on are placed in positions where there is potential for success.	☐	☐

If the people you select to be on your team are not successful, you will not be successful.

If you need to improve your selection and placement practices – DO IT NOW!

Well trained employees make more effective team members

Well trained employees have confidence in their ability to contribute to the team effort. They understand why it is important to help support other members of the team.

Resources such as knowledge of the needs of the organisation and control of work assignments are often available only to supervisors.

Any manager interested in improving team performance will ensure that training for each team member is appropriate.

The suggestions on the next page will help you to assess your current attitude and approach to training.

CHAPTER 14
Make Training Useful

Are you an effective trainer? Your attitude, knowledge and approach will influence what is learned and how well it is applied. Here are some suggestions to improve the return on investment in training for all concerned.

Place a ☑ if you already do what is suggested and an ☒ if you plan to begin this practice.

I normally:

☐ 1. Review performance against expectations with each employee periodically, and jointly identify training that will strengthen results.

☐ 2. Listen to an employee's career development objectives, and support them when it is appropriate to do so.

☐ 3. Talk in advance to employees selected for training to reinforce the importance of the training to their job.

☐ 4. Have employees' work covered by others while they are training so they can concentrate on what is being taught.

☐ 5. Help employees to develop an action plan to apply their training to the job.

☐ 6. Ask each trained employee for an evaluation of the training programme and whether it would be suitable for other members of the team.

☐ 7. Assign work to employees that allows them to apply new techniques and methods learned during training.

☐ 8. Compliment employees when they apply their newly acquired skills.

Team members must be committed to organisational goals

Your management style can help to focus employee efforts to achieve organisational goals.

The next page describes three different approaches to management. Which best fits you?

CHAPTER 15
Employee Focus and Commitment

☐ I know best

This person feels work should be done by controlling the people who do it. Employees are told what to do, how to do it, and when to stop. Then they are told what they did wrong and what they did right; where they are weak, and where they are strong. The person in charge feels this is justified because of his or her superior knowledge and ability. This attitude does not invite new ideas, challenge people, or stimulate a cooperative, supportive spirit. Communication is directed one way only.

☐ I'll set the goals, you meet them

This person feels that because of his or her superior knowledge, ability or experience it is all right to establish goals for others to meet. The employee is given an opportunity to discuss ways to meet goals, but has no input into the actual performance objectives. When this happens commitment is more difficult to obtain from employees because their lack of involvement precludes a sense of ownership.

☐ Let's review the work together

The leader who says, 'Let's establish more realistic goals and evaluate performance accordingly' emphasises work performance, not authoritarian control. The idea is first to communicate organisational needs, then help team members contribute their ideas. The leader acts as a resource and enabler rather than as a judge. Communication is open and flows in both directions. The value of mutual support and cooperation is recognised and employed.

Did you tick ☑ the one most like you?

CHAPTER 16
Make Commitment Possible

Supervisors cannot do it all, no matter how talented and committed they may be. Their success is measured by the ability to delegate intelligently and then motivate employees to accomplish the goals of the organisation. The highest level of achievement is attained when a team is committed to the task, and full use is made of each member's talents.

Commitment cannot be forced. It is self-generating and usually develops through a feeling of involvement. People increase commitment to a team when they are allowed to contribute to its success. Once actively involved in goal setting and problem-solving, a sense of ownership is developed. Team goals can be effectively pursued. Employees feel more important and entrepreneurial (and needed) when they have responsibility for results. This is the time a genuine concern is developed for other team members. Group problems become individual problems, and team goals become individual goals. Members contribute their best to problem-solving because they have a personal stake in doing so.

When members help to design the systems and methods used by the team, they understand why controls are important and make a commitment to support them. This is especially true when they know it is possible to revise or improve controls when required.

Involvement also helps team members to satisfy the participative needs of others. It builds a framework in which individual member needs can be learned, understood and supported by all.

A supervisor controls the degree to which employees are involved. Open up opportunities for participation and watch the commitment grow.

Involve team members individually and corporately

A *goal* is a statement of results to be achieved. Goals describe (1) conditions that will exist when the desired outcome has been accomplished; (2) a time frame during which the outcome is to be completed; and (3) resources the organisation is willing to commit to achieve the desired result.

A *standard* refers to a criterion of performance that must be met time and again. Standards are usually expressed quantitatively, and refer to such things as attendance, breakage, manufacturing tolerances, production rates and safety standards.

Goals and standards should be challenging but achievable. They should be established with the participation of those responsible for meeting them. After all, well selected, trained employees should know more about what is achievable than anyone else.

See the next page for some 'how to' suggestions.

CHAPTER 17

Involve the Team in Setting Goals and Standards

Here is one way team members can help to establish goals and standards and the action plans necessary to achieve them. Like other critical skills, goal setting may take practice.

The roles of the team member and the leader are outlined below. Tick those concepts with which you agree and are willing to try.

Team member	Leader
☐ Helps to establish performance goals and standards. This is a 'self-contract' for achievement as well as a commitment to deliver a result for the team.	☐ Ensures team goals are achievable, but challenging enough to meet organisational needs and provide a sense of accomplishment.
☐ Develops methods to measure results, and checkpoints for control purposes.	☐ Helps to balance the complexity of measures and controls with value received.
☐ Outlines the action required to accomplish goals and standards.	☐ Participates with the team to test the action plan's validity against other alternatives.

☐ Specifies participation required from colleagues or in other units within the organisation.

☐ Reviews what cooperation and support are required and helps to obtain them if necessary.

☐ Reports progress as work is performed. Seeks guidance and assistance when needed. Adjusts plan as required.

☐ Follows the progress of the work. Reinforces achievement and assists in problem-solving when indicated. Ensures targets are met, or modified if circumstances so indicate.

These roles place the responsibility for performance on the appropriate team members, and provide the latitude to achieve results. The leader concentrates on being a challenger, prober, coach and enabler.

Pass to employees problems which rightfully belong to them

Many supervisors spend too much time solving problems that could be better handled by individuals. When supervisors feel responsible for solving all the problems, production is slowed, employees are frustrated, and personal development is limited. The supervisor ends up with less time to plan, organise, motivate and control.

Team effectiveness is more easily achieved when the supervisor simply participates in problem-solving rather than dominating it.

CHAPTER 18
Teach Employees Problem-solving Techniques

Problem-solving should be taught at every level of an organisation. The process should be as simple as is required to get the job done. One basic approach is outlined below. Tick those steps that would be useful in your operation.

☐ **Step 1. State what appears to be the problem**
The real problem may not surface until facts have been gathered and analysed. Therefore, start with a supposition that can later be confirmed or corrected.

☐ **Step 2. Gather facts, feelings and opinions**
What happened? Where, when and how did it occur? What is its size, scope, and severity? Who and what is affected? Is it likely to happen again? Does it need to be corrected? Time and expense may require problem-solvers to think through what they need, and assign priorities to the more critical elements.

☐ **Step 3. Restate the problem**
The facts help to make this possible, and provide supporting data. The actual problem may or may not be the same as stated in step 1.

☐ **Step 4. Identify alternative solutions**
Generate ideas. Do not eliminate any possible solutions until several have been discussed.

☐ **Step 5. Evaluate alternatives**
Which will provide the optimum solution? What are the

risks? Are costs in keeping with the benefits? Will the solution create new problems?

☐ **Step 6. Implement the decision**
Who must be involved? To what extent? How, when and where? Who will the decision affect? What might go wrong? How will results be reported and verified?

☐ **Step 7. Evaluate the results**
Test the solution against the desired results. Modify the solution if better results are needed.

CHAPTER 19

Conditions which Support Effective Problem-solving by Teams

Improved results can be obtained from a team involved in problem-solving techniques when sound group processes are used. Team members are committed to finding the best possible solution to a problem rather than impose their exclusive view. The leader participates as a team member and is subject to the same rules. Open communication is expected, and team members are encouraged to challenge ideas in order to test their usefulness to solve the problem. A successful solution from a group is often far more effective than single solutions offered by individuals.

The following conditions support good team problem-solving. Tick ☑ those conditions now existing in your team and place an ☒ by those you want to add in the future.

☐ 1. Team members readily contribute from their experience and *listen* to the contributions of others.

☐ 2. Conflicts arising from different points of view are considered helpful and are resolved constructively by the team.

☐ 3. Team members challenge suggestions they believe are unsupported by facts or logic, but avoid arguing just to have their way.

☐ 4. Poor solutions are not supported just for the sake of harmony or agreement.

☐ 5. Differences of opinion are discussed and resolved. Coin tossing, averaging, majority vote and similar cop-outs are avoided when making a decision.

☐   6.   Every team member strives to make the problem-solving process efficient and is careful to facilitate rather than hinder discussion.

☐   7.   Team members encourage and support co-workers who may be reluctant to offer ideas.

☐   8.   Team members understand the value of time and work and so eliminate extraneous and/or repetitious discussion.

☐   9.   Team decisions are not arbitrarily overruled by the leader simply because he or she does not agree with them.

☐   10.   The team understands the leader will make the best decision he or she can, if a satisfactory team solution is not forthcoming.

CHAPTER 20
The Complaining Employees

Case 3

Joyce and Sue work in computer services under the supervision of Janice Johns. They are both depressed about their jobs and have been complaining to each other. Joyce is unhappy because she has never seen a description of her job and has only a limited understanding of what is expected of her. When she asked Janice about it, she was told, 'Don't worry, I'll keep you busy.' Joyce never receives a new assignment until she completes the previous one. Sometimes a day or more will pass before Janice is able to give Joyce a new project. Recently Joyce starting helping a co-worker because she had nothing else to do. Janice later told her: 'Don't do that again. Assignment of the work is my responsibility.' Joyce has since been criticised by her co-workers for not pitching in when they are busy and she is not.

Sue on the other hand, is concerned about the back-log building up in her job. The problem occurred because of repeated changes in project objectives which were not communicated until after a critical point in the work affected had been passed. Janice insists on personally handling all communications with other groups serviced by their department. Because Janice is so busy, she frequently fails to pass important information along to Sue and is equally slow in getting answers from Sue which are needed by others.

Are Sue's and Joyce's complaints justified? Yes ___ No ___

Support your position: _____

_____

_____

See page 84 for the author's ideas.

CHAPTER 21

Collaboration as a Source of Power in Team Building

Once you have a qualified staff, properly trained and focused on organisational goals, you have accomplished a great deal, but you still have not finished.

You must concentrate on building an atmosphere conducive to open communication, cooperation and trust, not only within your team, but also between your team and other units of the organisation.

Bringing team members together to collaborate on projects of mutual interest, and to generate ideas and suggestions for improvement of productivity, is one way to do this.

Collaboration has many benefits when it is used well. In the list below, tick those advantages of importance to you.

☐   Collaboration builds an awareness of interdependence. When people recognise the benefits of helping one another, and realise it is expected, they will work together to achieve common goals. The effort is non-threatening.

☐   When people work together to achieve common goals they stimulate each other to higher levels of accomplishment. Fresh ideas are generated and tested, and the team's productivity exceeds any combined efforts of employees working individually.

☐   Collaboration builds and reinforces recognition and mutual support within a team. People have an opportunity to see the effect of their effort and the efforts of others on achievement.

☐ Collaboration leads to commitment to support and accomplish organisational goals. People gain personal power in the form of confidence when they know others share their views and are acting in concert with them.

The benefits of collaboration make it easy to understand why managers who can make it happen are considered leaders. Collaboration can be encouraged and supported in the following ways. Tick those you plan to use.

☐ Identify areas of interdependence that make collaboration appropriate. Involve team members in planning and problem-solving to help them identify where collaboration is needed.

☐ Keep lines of communication open between everyone involved in a problem, project or course of action.

☐ Let the team know in advance that teamwork will positively influence individual recognition.

CHAPTER 22
Facilitate Open Communication

A leader uses communication to gather, process and transmit information essential to the well being of the organisation. Since this communication moves in many directions, leaders must carefully consider the needs of peers, superiors and team members.

The diagram on the next page reflects some important communication needs. If they are not met, team results will suffer.

The team leader can often facilitate communications by responding to the information needs of the organisation. Some typical examples are shown opposite.

Sending and listening skills are essential to good communication

The clarity with which signals are sent may make the difference between winning and losing.

Research shows that the best leaders are good communicators. They have learned to give clear instructions; stay responsive to questions and suggestions; and keep the appropriate parties well informed.

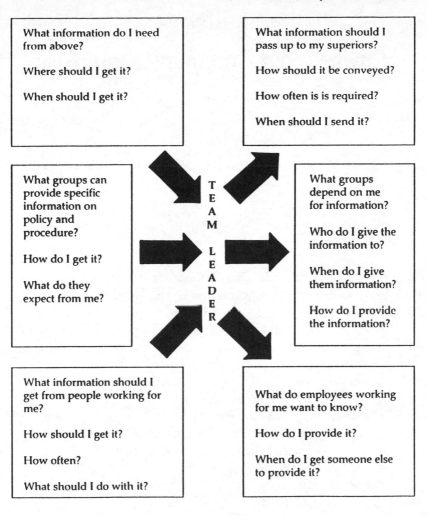

What information do I need from above?

Where should I get it?

When should I get it?

What information should I pass up to my superiors?

How should it be conveyed?

How often is is required?

When should I send it?

What groups can provide specific information on policy and procedure?

How do I get it?

What do they expect from me?

TEAM LEADER

What groups depend on me for information?

Who do I give the information to?

When do I give them information?

How do I provide the information?

What information should I get from people working for me?

How should I get it?

How often?

What should I do with it?

What do employees working for me want to know?

How do I provide it?

When do I get someone else to provide it?

Research also confirms a positive correlation between communication (understanding) and:

- improved productivity
- better problem-solving
- a reduction in grievances
- ideas for improvement in methodology
- improved working relationships
- greater personal satisfaction.

CHAPTER 23
Review Your Communication Skills

Complete each of the following statements by circling the most appropriate choice.

1. Messages are the most easily understood when:
   (a) you use your full command of the language.
   (b) they are sent in terms the receiver understands.
2. Complex information is more easily understood when you:
   (a) improve clarity by using specific examples and analogies.
   (b) tell the listener to pay careful attention.
3. Key concepts are better remembered when you:
   (a) use repetition to reinforce them.
   (b) express yourself clearly.
4. Organising a message before transmitting it:
   (a) often takes more time than it is worth.
   (b) makes it easier to understand.
5. The sender can assess the receiver's understanding by:
   (a) asking if he or she understands.
   (b) asking the receiver to report what he or she heard.
6. Listening is more effective when you:
   (a) concentrate on the sender and what is being said.
   (b) anticipate what the speaker is going to say.
7. Understanding is easier when you:
   (a) suspend judgement until the sender finishes the message.
   (b) assume you know the sender's position and judge accordingly.

8. Understanding can be improved by the listener:
   (a) periodically paraphrasing the messge back to the sender.
   (b) interrupting to express feelings and emotions.
9. Good listeners:
   (a) have their response ready when the sender stops talking.
   (b) ask questions when they don't understand.
10. Sending and receiving are both enhanced when:
    (a) the parties maintain good eye contact.
    (b) the parties are defensive and challenge one another.

Encourage team members to review communication skill using this same exercise. Then compare notes and discuss how to improve. This will be another cooperative step in building a stronger team effort.

Answers:
1(b); 2(a); 3(a); 4(b); 5(b); 6(a); 7(a); 8(a); 9(b); 10(a).

CHAPTER 24
Understand Conflict

Team leaders must accept the fact that any time two or more people are brought together, the stage is set for potential conflict. When conflict does occur, the results may be positive or negative depending upon how those involved choose to approach it.

With this in mind, team leaders must be sensitive to the fact that positive contributions can arise from conflict provided things do not get out of control. Teaching team members to understand conflict and resolve it positively will help the team to succeed. The next few pages offer some tips on conflict management.

Some members of Memorial Church want to use church funds to aid the local unemployed. Others prefer spending more money for missionary work. Still others think new carpeting for the sanctuary is the greatest need.

A sales manager wants a large stock of all products so that customers can be promised quick deliveries. The manufacturing manager wants to limit stock to hold down storage costs.

In both these situations everyone means well, and if questioned would maintain they were trying to accomplish what they perceive to be the best objective. None the less, conflict is present because of:

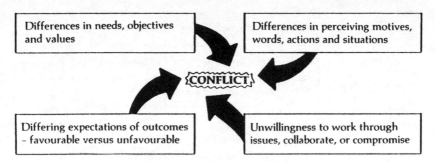

Conflict becomes unhealthy when it is avoided or approached on a win/lose basis (one party only can win, the other only lose). Animosities will develop, communications will break down, trust and mutual support will deteriorate, and hostilities result. When sides are chosen productivity will diminish or stop. The damage is usually difficult (sometimes impossible) to repair.

Conflict is healthy when it causes the parties to explore new ideas, test their position and beliefs, and stretch their imagination. When conflict is dealt with constructively, people can be stimulated to greater creativity, which will lead to a wider choice of action and better results.

Conflict resolution

There are five basic approaches to conflict resolution, shown overleaf. They can be summarised as follows. Indicate the one you are most likely to use with followers with an F ; your peers a P ; and with your supervisor an S .

Style	Characteristic behaviour	User justification
Avoidance ☐ ☐ ☐	Non-confrontational. Ignores or passes over issues. Denies issues are a problem.	Differences too minor or too great to resolve. Attempts might damage relationships or create even greater problems.
Accommodating ☐ ☐ ☐	Agreeable, non-assertive behaviour. Cooperative even at the expense of personal goals.	Not worth risking damage to relationships or general disharmony.
Win/Lose ☐ ☐ ☐	Confrontational, assertive and aggressive. Must win at any cost.	Survival of the fittest. Must prove superiority. Most ethically or professionally correct.
Compromising ☐ ☐ ☐	Important all parties achieve basic goals and maintain good relationships. Aggressive but cooperative.	No one person or idea is perfect. There is more than one good way to do anything. You must give to get.
Problem-solving ☐ ☐ ☐	Needs of both parties are legitimate and important. High respect for mutual support. Assertive and cooperative.	When parties will openly discuss issues, a mutually beneficial solution can be found without anyone making a major concession.

Review the chart with team members. Share the answers to test each other's perceptions. Discuss ways that conflicts can be more effectively resolved in the team and with other units.

You and your team may find the following diagram helpful in discussing conflict resolution styles.

Answer the following questions:

1. Which style is the most uncooperative and least assertive?

   _____

2. Which style is characterised by assertive behaviour, yet represents the maximum in cooperation? _____

3. Which style is totally cooperative but unassertive? _____

4. Which style is totally assertive and uncooperative? _____

5. Which style takes the middle ground on assertiveness and cooperation? _____

When team members understand the nature of conflict and constructive methods to resolve it, they can usually work out disagreements themselves. When they can't, or when the problem requires your intervention for other reasons, you may have to engineer a solution.

Test your skill at this by solving the case on the next page.

Answers to questions:
1. Avoidance; 2. Problem-solving; 3. Accommodating; 4. Win/Lose; 5. Compromising.

CHAPTER 25
Resolving Conflict

Case 4

Justin is supervisor of a small group of quality control testers in a chemical products laboratory. At different times, two testers have come to him with different suggestions for reporting test results to plant operations. The first, Robert, wants to send the results to the foreman in charge of the unit where the samples were produced. Ginny, on the other hand, wants to send the reports directly to the lead operator on the unit so corrective changes can be made as soon as possible. Ginny and Robert are both good people but very competitive. Justin is aware they have already exchanged a few sharp remarks over the issue. Both ideas are reasonable and either is better than the current practice of sending reports to the administrative office.

In the choices below, identify the five basic approaches to conflict resolution in the blank provided. Then indicate with a tick ☑ the approach you would use if you were Justin.

☐ 1. _____ Study the situation independently, decide who is right, and tell Robert and Ginny to implement your decision.

☐ 2. _____ Wait to see what happens.

☐ 3. _____ Let each handle their reporting their way.

☐ 4. _____ Get Robert and Ginny together to work out a solution they can both live with, even though they must both give a little.

☐ 5. _____ Suggest Robert and Ginny combine their ideas so that both can achieve their goals (send the report to the foreman with a copy to the lead operator).

Compare your answers with those of the author on page 84.

As people work through the team building processes, they get to know each other. They learn to respect individual differences, appreciate team contributions, and enjoy the satisfaction teamwork provides when both personal and organisational goals are achieved.

Trust is an essential part of this experience. It is important because of the powerful effect it has on every aspect of team performance.

Over the years, the author of this book has asked participants in workshops to write down their feelings about trust. A few are shown on the following page.

CHAPTER 26
Building Trust in Teams

The following statements are actual responses of individuals who learned team building techniques.

Individual

A

To build trust it is essential to have clearly and consistently administered goals which contain employee input. Employees must perceive their managers as open, fair, honest and willing to listen. Managers must be decisive and stand by their decisions in difficult situations.

Employees must have the confidence that their manager will support them, even in delicate matters, and take responsibility for group actions. A manager must also readily give credit to employees where credit is due.

B

I define trust as an assured reliance on the character, ability, and strength or truth of someone or something. Trust is built in a work group by promoting open communication, providing fair leadership, and supervising with sensitivity.

C	Establishing trust in a work group requires open and honest communication, accepting others, sharing a common goal, and respecting the opinions of others on how to achieve that goal.
D	Trust is necessary for a productive working environment. It is essential for all personnel to practise open, honest communication in order to increase awareness and build cooperation. This environment of trust promotes loyalty and commitment to achieve the goals and objectives of the organisation.

Praise is priceless

When communication is open, conflict is resolved positively, and mutual support and trust have been achieved, you are in sight of success. Your team's performance should be appropriately recognised.

There are many forms of recognition, but one of the most powerful is praise. Some managers use praise effectively, others use it poorly or not at all. See the next page for some successes and failures.

CHAPTER 27
Which Will You Be?

Successes	Failures
Leaders who think it important to help people feel good about themselves.	Those who are insensitive to the needs of others.
Leaders who give periodic praise to team members for meeting job requirements.	Those who think praise is improper for persons who meet, but do not exceed, job requirements.
Leaders who understand that people respond better to praise of what they do well than by criticism of what they do wrong.	Those who look only for what is being done wrong and consistently give only negative feedback.
Leaders who give sincere praise for reasons the receiver can understand.	Those who are insincere and use praise only to get something they want.
Leaders who praise teamwork but also recognise individual contributions to final results.	Those who do not go to the trouble to reward teamwork or identify individual contributions.

Add from your own
experience:

_____

_____

_____

_____

Add from your own
experience:

_____

_____

_____

_____

Praise given when earned rewards the giver as well as the
receiver.

Teams can profit from feedback

Team performance can be improved when members provide
feedback on how well things are being done. Positive recognition
when things are done correctly encourages similar performance
in the future. Corrective action to redirect inappropriate or
inadequate performance clears the air and can set the stage for
future success.

You have just reviewed some positive approaches to praise. On
the facing page see how corrective action can also be taken using
positive methods.

CHAPTER 28
Accentuate the Positive

Discipline is a basic requirement of team performance. A good leader maintains control but strives to establish an environment in which team members will exercise self-control. This is accomplished by following through on the true meaning of discipline, namely, 'training that develops or moulds by instruction or exercise'. The means by which positive discipline can be implemented are listed below. Indicate your proficiency with each technique by ticking the appropriate box.

Technique	Do well	Should improve
1. From the outset, make sure team members understand what is expected of them and what standards are to be met.	☐	☐
2. Teach team members how to fulfil expectations and achieve standards.	☐	☐
3. Encourage team members as they make progress towards attaining company goals.	☐	☐
4. Compliment team members when standards are achieved and expectations are realised.	☐	☐
5. Redirect inadequate or inappropriate performance when it occurs, and repeat 1–4.	☐	☐

6. If the inadequate or inappropriate ☐ ☐
   performance persists after a reasonable
   period of time (and step 5 has been
   applied), retire or transfer the player. He
   or she hasn't made the team.

This process, when consistently applied and followed, will eliminate most disciplinary problems. If you have not been doing this, you can institute it immediately with your entire team. Most people want to do the right thing but they often need guidance to know what that is.

CHAPTER 29
Coaching:
A Key Ingredient in Team Building

Forming a team, developing the personal skills of its members and enabling them to work together effectively are only the initial steps in team building. These first steps must be sustained by continuous analysis of results and corresponding adjustments in member contributions and the game plan to meet changing objectives. The team leader, therefore, must be an adept coach who is constantly improving and applying coaching techniques to meet the needs of the situation and the team.

Most managers can identify people who have influenced their lives in some particular way. The people involved may include parents, friends, teachers, associates or supervisors. In some instances, this influence has been profound, perhaps even changing the course of their lives.

Think about it and make some notes in the space provided.

Who influenced you?

_____

_____

_____

_____

In what way were you influenced?

_____

_____

_____

Would you be who you are today without those influences?

Yes ____   No ____

Who influences you now?

_____

_____

_____

_____

What outcomes do you have the power to influence?

_____

_____

More reasons why coaching is important

Few people who achieve a position of leadership can truly claim sole responsibility for their accomplishment. Someone helped them. Someone who knew the goals of the organisation and the individual, and who was willing to devote some effort to the need satisfaction of both, was active in their life.

This action may have been so subtle, so natural, so well organised, or so well woven into the fabric of the relationship, that it is visible only in retrospect. Managers who have this kind of positive impact on others in their team recognise that the helping relationship is fundamental to the development of a strong organisation.

In this role of helping people to grow and adjust to change, the manager is a coach. He or she provides guidance and support but realises that the employee must also help him/herself.

The manager must not only realise that helping is a basic function of supervision, but must also let team members know that he or she is available and wants to help them. Sometimes this help comes in the form of reassurance and empathy. Sometimes it just involves listening and reflecting. But more importantly, coaching means giving people challenges, delegating responsibilities, giving them opportunities to get involved and to grow and develop by learning from their own successes and their own mistakes.

Managers who are committed to coaching see this function not as a luxury to be carried out when time permits, but as an absolute necessity. They have experienced the results that occur when employees are encouraged to work at their potential. They have enjoyed the increased productivity and appreciated the strengthening of their organisation as individuals begin to demonstrate their competence and improve their contribution to the team.

What is your attitude towards coaching?

Coaching offers one of the best opportunities you have to leave a positive imprint on individual team members, your team as a whole and the organisation. Some managers consider the coaching aspects of their jobs the most rewarding and lasting contributions they can make in the work setting.

What is your attitude towards coaching? Have you given it any constructive thought? Use the scale overleaf first to reflect your attitude towards coaching in the past. Then, after contemplating what you have learned from your personal experience and from reading this book, reflect what you anticipate your attitude towards coaching will be in the future.

Coaching applications	Former attitude towards coaching			Future attitude towards coaching		
	Essential	*Useful*	*Waste of time*	*Essential*	*Useful*	*Waste of time*
Coaching is vital to shaping employee performance in the current assignment.						
Coaching enables employees to learn more quickly and reach their level of competence more rapidly.						
Coaching provides a way to help employees achieve their potential as well as tailor that potential to support the skills of other team members.						
Employees accept and adapt more quickly to change when coaching involves them in the process and guides them through.						
Coaching following performance feedback improves the likelihood of positive results.						

Rate your skills as a coach

Rate your coaching effectiveness on the following scale. A 5 indicates you consider yourself outstanding; a 4, very good; a 3, satisfactory; a 2, needs improvement; a 1, poor. To check your ratings, ask your employees to rate you on the same scale.

1. I recognise differences in my staff and coach them accordingly.   5 4 3 2 1
2. I keep my employees informed about organisational plans and operating systems.   5 4 3 2 1
3. I encourage employee suggestions on the implementation of change.   5 4 3 2 1
4. I encourage employees to solve their own problems.   5 4 3 2 1
5. I make sure each employee has a continuing understanding of what is expected of him/her.   5 4 3 2 1
6. I am frank with employees about their performance.   5 4 3 2 1
7. I help employees to prepare for the future.   5 4 3 2 1
8. I give praise and other appropriate rewards to recognise achievement.   5 4 3 2 1
9. I keep employees focused on team effectiveness but make everyone aware of the value of their personal contributions.   5 4 3 2 1
10. I caution employees who fail consistently as team players and who do not respond to coaching.   5 4 3 2 1
11. I know the personal aspirations of each member of my team.   5 4 3 2 1
12. I look for ways to help people grow on the job.   5 4 3 2 1
13. I ask other team members to assist one another to learn and to grow.   5 4 3 2 1
14. I make sure team members understand that the success of our team and each of its members (myself included) depends on them.   5 4 3 2 1
15. I make myself available to the team and to individuals on a high priority basis.   5 4 3 2 1
16. I do not discourage conflict but I insist it be resolved in a timely manner.   5 4 3 2 1
17. I work hard to ensure that team members understand, respect and support one another.   5 4 3 2 1

18. I share my knowledge and expertise with the
    team and expect the same in return.   5 4 3 2 1

> If you scored less than four on any item, that practice should
> become a target for personal improvement.

The coaching process

The manager who wants to improve coaching skills can start by
focusing on what an employee needs to survive and to support
self-development. Here are some of these needs along with some
coaching methods that will provide appropriate help. Use them as
a checklist to measure how well you are doing and as a guide for
growth.

What employees need to develop themselves	Coaching methods to help an employee to grow and adjust to change

1. A basic understanding of his/her job and its contribution to the team.	1. A manager enables this by:
	  A. Developing with the employee what the job is, particularly basic functions and relationships.
	  B. Involving the employee in goal setting.
	  C. Jointly establishing standards for accuracy, punctuality, efficiency, etc.

2. A continuing understanding of what is expected from him or her.	2. A manager facilitates this by:
	  A. Keeping the employee aware of changes in objectives and organisational needs.
	  B. Helping the employee to understand the impact of change on job requirements, priorities and the future.

C. Developing with the employee how any unusual assignments will be completed in terms of importance, scope, timing, approach, facilities and other factors.

3. The opportunity to participate in planning change and to perform in keeping with ability.

3. A manager makes this possible by:
   A. Seeking and utilising employee ideas.
   B. Delegating appropriate tasks.
   C. Avoiding excessive supervision and decision making for the employee.
   D. Exercising less control as abilities and confidence improve.
   E. Accepting occasional mistakes as a part of the price of experience.

4. To receive assistance when needed.

4. A manager is coaching when he/she:
   A. Encourages questions and reviews job-related problems when help is needed.
   B. Provides assistance when critical problems arise.
   C. Makes decisions beyond an employee's authority when necessary.

5. To know how well he/she is doing.

5. A manager communicates how well the employee is doing by:
   A. Frequently reviewing results in relation to objectives, agreed standards and changing needs. Giving the employee appropriate feedback.
   B. Discussing performance in terms of future development every six months.

6. To be recognised and rewarded based on his/her performance.

6. A manager supports employee performance and growth by:
   A. Expressing appreciation and providing other recognition at the most appropriate time.
   B. Commending sustained satisfactory work.
   C. Recommending or not recommending promotion or reassignment.

7. To work in a climate which encourages self-development.

7. A manager creates this environment by:
   A. Establishing a relationship with each employee based on mutual confidence.
   B. Encouraging and using suggestions and ideas.
   C. Keeping each employee currently informed of things which affect him/her and the work group.
   D. Backing up employees with higher management.
   E. Sharing personal philosophies.

As each employee grows through coaching, it is also the responsibility of the coach (manager) to integrate the new skills continuously into effective team performance that supports organisational and personal goals to the maximum possible.

CHAPTER 30
Reading Review

It's time now to measure your progress. Which of the following statements are true and which false?

True   **False**

_____ _____ 1. Team leaders emphasise each member's involvement and expect that person to take responsibility for his or her contribution.

_____ _____ 2. If you plan to build a strong team and use members' skills to the maximum, there is little need to improve your own skills.

_____ _____ 3. People are more productive when they feel a sense of ownership of the task or of the organisation.

_____ _____ 4. When a true team achieves success, so will all of its members.

_____ _____ 5. Selecting qualified people who work well with others at the outset supports team building.

_____ _____ 6. Commitment to task accomplishment results when a leader involves team members in planning, goal setting and problem-solving.

_____ _____ 7. Team leaders facilitate training for team members and coach them to apply what has been learned.

_____ _____ 8. Teams are more concerned with getting positive results than they are with demarcation disputes.

_____ _____ 9. Trust is a minor factor in most team situations.

_____ _____ 10. Team members need to know everything that affects the work they are performing.

_____ _____ 11. Competition and conflict in a team are healthy if they are properly controlled and quickly resolved.

_____ _____ 12. Open communication in a team will promote understanding and recognition of individual differences, and encourage mutual support.

_____ _____ 13. Teams participate in decision-making but recognise that their leader must act on his or her own if consensus cannot be reached or there is a crisis.

_____ _____ 14. Successful teams have little need for recognition and praise.

_____ _____ 15. Self-control and good discipline are by-products of team building.

Check your answers with the author's on page 79.

Reading review answers

1. True.   Involvement and responsibility are critical to teams.
2. False.   This is one of the most challenging times ever for leaders.
3. True.   Ownership builds commitment and responsibility.
4. True.   Success indicates everyone played their role.
5. True.   Good people are the foundation for success.
6. True.   You can't demand it or force it.
7. True.   Leaders make training useful.
8. True.   Productivity, commitment, open communication and trust are the usual casualties of departmental wars.
9. False.   Trust is one of the most vital ingredients.
10. True.   The right information makes the job easier.
11. True.   It is stimulating and mind opening.
12. True.   Forget this principle at your own risk.
13. True.   Timeliness is also important in decision-making.
14. False. Recognition and praise are among the strongest motivators known.
15. True.   People who are committed to a task, a unit and each other are not apt to create unnecessary problems.

CHAPTER 31
Ten Unforgivable Mistakes

Don't get trapped by the ten unforgivable mistakes listed below.

Tick those you intend to avoid.

☐ 1. Failure to develop and maintain basic management and leadership skills.

☐ 2. Permitting poor employee selection techniques.

☐ 3. Failure to discuss expectations or establish goals which have been mutually set.

☐ 4. Inattention to the training and development needs of team members.

☐ 5. Failure to advocate, support and nurture team building activities.

☐ 6. Preventing the involvement of team members in any activity where they could make a contribution.

☐ 7. Failure to provide and receive feedback from the team.

☐ 8. Allowing conflict and competition to get out of control, or trying to eliminate it altogether.

☐ 9. Depending on someone else to recognise and reward the team and its members.

☐ 10. Failure to send players who have not responded to coaching back to the B team.

CHAPTER 32
Develop a Personal Action Plan

Think over the material you have read. Review the self-analysis questionnaires. Rethink the case studies and the reinforcement exercises. What have you learned about team building? What did you learn about yourself? How can you apply what you learned? Make a commitment to yourself to become a better team player and a more effective team builder by designing a personal action plan to help you accomplish this goal.

The following guide may help to clarify your goals and outline actions required to achieve them.

1. My current team building skills are effective in the following areas:

   _____

   _____

   _____

2. I need to improve my team building skills in the following areas:

   _____

   _____

   _____

3. My goals for improving my team building skills are as follows: (Be sure they are specific, attainable and measurable.)

_____

_____

_____

4. These people and resources can help me to achieve my goals.

_____

_____

5. Below are my action steps, along with a timetable to accomplish each goal.

_____

_____

_____

CHAPTER 33
Answers to Cases

Case 1. Can this supervisor be saved? (page 22)
Marilyn is in serious trouble. It will take real effort to turn things around. It appears that Marilyn is trapped by her office and her paperwork. She needs training to develop better competence and more confidence as a supervisor. Until she learns to manage herself, she will be unable to manage anyone else. Her employees also seem untrained, unsure of themselves and poorly disciplined. Until they understand their jobs better and recognise the importance of cooperating with each other, chaos will be the result.

Since Marilyn's group is interdependent it must work as a team to be successful. Marilyn must try her best to learn and apply team concepts. Specifically, she must become a better leader and supervisor; build the skills and confidence of her employees; establish a better working climate; and institute an appropriate reward system. How to accomplish this is the basis of this book.

Case 2. Which supervisor would you prefer? (page 32)
It is good that both Moira and Jeff recognise the importance of clear goals and plans. Employees who have limited knowledge or expertise may appreciate Moira's approach because they have a great deal to learn. As they learn under Moira's management, however, they may feel too restricted to share their ideas. New methods, better products and simpler ways to achieve objectives might not be forthcoming. Experienced employees may feel that way at the outset.

Experienced employees will appreciate Jeff's approach because it provides a needed outlet to contribute. They will feel free to improve the effectiveness of the group while improving their own. Employees with lesser skills will be encouraged to learn so they too can become more productive and contribute. Jeff's employees will appreciate his decision to participate in supervisory training because they appreciate a manager who knows the basics.

Case 3. The complaining employees (page 48)

Joyce and Sue have good reasons to complain. Joyce wants the opportunity to grow beyond her current tasks. Her efforts to learn what is expected of her have been blocked, and she is discouraged by waiting for assignments. She has been told not to worry about being idle and instructed not to help others unless so directed. This is frustrating for people who want to contribute.

Sue is suffering the consequences of poor communication from her supervisor. This is an impossible situation for Sue to correct until Janice either opens communication channels between users and Sue, or begins relaying information promptly.

Janice appears to be over-controlling her employees by assuming they cannot think for themselves. She is also preventing voluntary attempts by employees to help and support one another. Janice needs to re-evaluate her approach to supervision and be more open in her dealings with employees; otherwise Janice will soon be an 'ex-manager'.

Case 4. Resolving conflict (page 61)

Using a *win/lose* approach (item 1) takes a problem-solving opportunity away from Ginny and Robert and makes one of them a loser. *Avoidance* (item 2) leaves two recommendations unresolved. *Accommodation* (item 3) may work, but could be confusing for the operating department. *Compromising* (item 4) might be the best solution in this instance because it requires each employee to examine his or her thinking carefully in the light of the other's arguments, and work together to reach an agreeable decision. During this process, they may end up using item 5, *problem-solving*, because it not only gets the job done, it also satisfies the recommendation each made originally.